# CREEDS

of

# Life, Love, & Inspiration

A Guidebook of Everyday
Wisdom & Thought

**Blue Mountain Press** ®

Boulder, Colorado

Library of Congress Catalog Card Number: 99-35839
ISBN: 0-88396-523-2

ACKNOWLEDGMENTS appear on page 64.

**H** design on book cover is registered in the U.S. Patent and Trademark Office.

Manufactured in the United States of America
First Printing in Hardcover: June 1999

♺ This book is printed on recycled paper.

**Library of Congress Cataloging-in-Publication Data**

Creeds of life, love & inspiration : a guidebook of everyday
    wisdom & thought / [compiled by Blue Mountain Arts].
        p.   cm.
        ISBN 0-88396-523-2 (alk. paper). -- ISBN 0-88396-520-8 (pbk. : alk. paper)
        1. Conduct of life Quotations, maxims, etc.  I. Blue Mountain Arts
    (Firm) II. Title: Creeds of life, love and inspiration.
    PN6084.C556C74    1999
    082--dc21                                                        99-35839
                                                                            CIP

# Blue Mountain Press INC.

P.O. Box 4549, Boulder, Colorado 80306

# CONTENTS

# May You Always
# Have an Angel by Your Side

May you always have an angel by your side ◦ Watching
out for you in all the things you do ◦ Reminding you to keep
believing in brighter days ◦ Finding ways for your wishes and
dreams to take you to beautiful places ◦ Giving you hope that
is as certain as the sun ◦ Giving you the strength of serenity
as your guide ◦ May you always have love and comfort and
courage ◦

And may you always have an angel by your side ◦ Someone
there to catch you if you fall ◦ Encouraging your dreams ◦
Inspiring your happiness ◦ Holding your hand and helping you
through it all ◦

In all of our days, our lives are always changing ◦ Tears come
along as well as smiles ◦ Along the roads you travel, may the
miles be a thousand times more lovely than lonely ◦ May
they give you gifts that never, ever end: someone wonderful
to love and a dear friend in whom you can confide ◦ May
you have rainbows after every storm ◦ May you have hopes
to keep you warm ◦

◦ And may you always have an angel by your side ◦

— Douglas Pagels

# A Creed to Live By

Don't undermine your worth by comparing yourself with others. It is because we are different that each of us is special. Don't set your goals by what other people deem important. Only you know what is best for you. Don't take for granted the things closest to your heart. Cling to them as you would your life, for without them life is meaningless. Don't let your life slip through your fingers by living in the past or for the future. By living your life one day at a time, you live all the days of your life. Don't give up when you still have something to give. Nothing is really over until the moment you stop trying.

Don't be afraid to admit that you are less than perfect. It is this fragile thread that binds us to one another. Don't be afraid to encounter risks. It is by taking chances that we learn how to be brave. Don't shut love out of your life by saying it's impossible to find. The quickest way to receive love is to give love; the fastest way to lose love is to hold it too tightly; and the best way to keep love is to give it wings. Don't dismiss your dreams. To be without dreams is to be without hope; to be without hope is to be without purpose. Don't run through life so fast that you forget not only where you've been but also where you're going. Life is not a race, but a journey to be savored each step of the way.

— Nancye Sims

# Make Love a Part
# of Everything You Do

Special people are those
who have the ability to share
    their lives with others.
They are honest in word and deed,
they are sincere and compassionate,
and they always make sure that
    love is a part of everything.

Special people are those who have the ability
to give to others
and help them with the changes
    that come their way.
They are not afraid
of being vulnerable;
they believe in their uniqueness
    and are proud to be who they are.
Special people are those who
allow themselves the pleasures
of being close to others
    and caring about their happiness.
They have come to understand
that love is what makes
    the difference in life.

— Deanna Beisser

# Love

Love takes time. It needs a history of giving
and receiving, laughing and crying...
Love never promises instant gratification, only
ultimate fulfillment.
Love means believing in someone, in something.
It supposes a willingness to struggle, to work,
to suffer, and to rejoice.
Satisfaction and ultimate fulfillment are
by-products of dedicated love. They belong only
to those who can reach beyond themselves; to
whom giving is more important than receiving.
Love is doing everything you can to help others
build whatever dreams they have.
Love involves much careful and active listening.
It is doing whatever needs to be done, and
saying whatever will promote the other's
happiness, security, and well-being. Sometimes,
love hurts.
Love is on a constant journey to what others
need. It must be attentive, caring, and open,
both to what others say and to what others
cannot say.
Love says no with empathy and great compassion.
Love is firm, but when needed it must be tender.

When others have tried and failed, love is the
    hand in yours in your moments of
    discouragement and disappointment.
Love is reliable.
Love is a choice and commitment to others' true
    and lasting happiness. It is dedicated to growth
    and fulfillment. Love is not selfish.
Love sometimes fails for lack of wisdom or
    abundance of weakness, but it forgives, knowing
    the intentions are good.
Love does not attach conditions... Genuine love is
    always a free gift.
Love realizes and accepts that there will be
    disagreements and disturbing emotions...
    There may be times when miles lie between,
    but love is a commitment. It believes, and
    endures all things.
Love encourages freedom of self. Love shares
    positive and negative reactions to warm and
    cold feelings.
Love, intimate love, will never reject others. It is
    the first to encourage and the last to condemn.
Love is a commitment to growth, happiness, and
    fulfillment of one another.

— Barb Upham

# You Can Be Whatever
# You Want to Be

There is inside you
all of the potential to be whatever
    you want to be —
all of the energy to do whatever
    you want to do.
Imagine yourself as you would like to be,
    doing what you want to do,
and each day, take one step
    toward your dream.
And though at times it may seem too
    difficult to continue,
hold on to your dream.
One morning you will awake to find
that you are the person
    you dreamed of —
doing what you wanted to do —
simply because you had the courage
to believe in your potential
and to hold on to your dream.

— Donna Levine

I expect to pass this way but once;
any good therefore that I can do,
or any kindness that I can show to
any fellow creature, let me do it now.
Let me not defer or neglect it,
for I shall not pass this way again.

— Etienne de Grellet

# The Serenity Prayer

God grant me the serenity
to accept the things
    I cannot change;
the courage to change
    the things I can;
and the wisdom
    to know the difference.

— Reinhold Niebuhr

# Believe in Yourself

Believe that you have the destiny, the innate ability, to become all you expect of life. Experience all of life's peaks and plateaus. Find the meaning of life's struggles and accomplishments. There you will find the meaning to life and life's work.

Trust in your deeply hidden feelings, because they show the person that you are. Take hold of each opportunity, and make the most of it.

Know the person that you are, the needs that your life contains. Search deeply to capture the essence of life. Find your limitations and build upon them. Create within yourself a person who is strong and capable of withstanding pain.

Know that life will offer some disappointments, but remember, through those situations you become a stronger, more stable person. Don't overlook obstacles, but work through them. Remember that each road you choose will offer some difficulty. If life were meant to be easy, there would be no challenges and no rainbows.

— Sherrie Householder

This life is yours
Take the power
to choose what you want to do
and do it well
Take the power
to love what you want in life
and love it honestly
Take the power
to walk in the forest
and be a part of nature
Take the power
to control your own life
No one else can do it for you
Take the power
to make your life
healthy
exciting
worthwhile
and very happy

— Susan Polis Schutz

It is easy enough to be pleasant,
    When life flows by like a song,
But the man worth while is one who will smile,
    When everything goes dead wrong.
For the test of the heart is trouble,
    And it always comes with the years,
And the smile that is worth the praises of earth,
    Is the smile that shines through tears.

— Ella Wheeler Wilcox

As human beings, we're not perfect,
and we're not supposed to be.
But that's not always
an easy thing for us to realize.
The best we can do
is to do the best we can,
give it our all, and always give thanks.
We don't make it alone in this world.
We're lucky that there are people
placed in our path to guide us,
protect us, and touch our lives
so that we can get through it all...
one day at a time.

— Julia Escobar

Take time to work —
it is the price of success.
Take time to think —
it is the source of power.
Take time to play —
it is the secret of perpetual youth.
Take time to read —
it is the foundation of wisdom.
Take time to be friendly —
it is the road to happiness.
Take time to dream —
it is hitching a wagon to a star.
Take time to love and be loved —
it is the privilege of the Gods.
Take time to look around —
the day is too short to be selfish.
Take time to laugh —
it is the music of the soul.

— Old Irish Prayer

# Life's Most Important Treasures

Joy
    in your heart,
    your mind,
    your soul.
Peace
    with yourself
    and with the universe.
Harmony.
Courage
    to feel, to need,
    to reach out.
Freedom
    to let yourself
    be bound by love.
Friendship.
Wisdom
    to learn, to change,
    to let go.
Acceptance
    of the truth
    and beauty within yourself.
Growth.
Pleasure
    in all that you see,
    and touch,
    and do.
Happiness
    with yourself
    and with the world.
Love.

— Maureen Doan

# There Is So Much to Be Thankful For

We don't often
take the time out of
our busy lives
to think about all
the beautiful things
and to be thankful for them
If we did
reflect on these things
we would realize how very
lucky and fortunate we really are

I am very thankful
for the love of my husband —
which is so complete and fulfilling
and is based on honesty, equality
intellectualism and romance

I am very thankful
for the love of my children —
which is all encompassing
and is based on teaching, tenderness
sensitivity, caring and hugging

I am very thankful
that I am able to love
and that the love is returned to me

I am very thankful
that I am healthy
and that the people I love
are healthy

I am very thankful
that I have dreams to follow
and goals to strive for

I am very thankful
for the beauty of nature —
magnificent mountains
the colorful leaves
the smell of the flowers
the roaring of the waves
the setting sun
the rising moon

Everywhere I look
I see the wonders of nature
and I feel so proud
to be a small part of it

I am very thankful
for all the good people in the world
I am very thankful
that I have good friends

I am very thankful
to be alive
in a time when
we can make the world
a better place
to live in

— Susan Polis Schutz

# What to Do When You're Feeling a Little Overwhelmed by It All...

Some days are better than others.
Some are a little bit worse.
Sometimes everything works out okay.
Sometimes you can't get past the hurts.

When things get a little too stressful and you wonder how
you'll make it through, you need to take everything
a day at a time, and do what works <u>for</u> <u>you</u>.

Find a place in your heart where you see the way through to the
truths about how things can be. Use your inner strength and your
quiet resolve and all your positive qualities. Know that you're in
the prayers of others. Whisper a few of your own. You don't have
to do it all by yourself. Rest assured that you're never alone.

You're a strong and special person. The very best is wished for you.
   Have faith that tomorrow will bring brighter days.
      And always have faith in... you.

— Marin McKay

# Let Go of the Past

Let go...
  of guilt; it's okay to make the same
  mistakes again.
Let go...
  of obsessions; they seldom
  turn out the way you planned.
Let go...
  of hate; it's a waste of love.
Let go...
  of blaming others; you are responsible
  for your own destiny.
Let go...
  of fantasies; so reality can come true.
Let go...
  of self-pity; someone else may need you.
Let go...
  of wanting; cherish what you have.
Let go...
  of fear; it's a waste of faith.
Let go...
  of despair; change comes from acceptance
  and forgiveness.
Let go...
  of the past; the future is here —
  right now.

— Kathleen O'Brien

# Be the Person
# You Were Meant to Be

You can be all the things you dream of being,
if you're willing to work hard
and if you believe in yourself more.
Learn from the mistakes of others —
accept them; forgive them.
Don't use the roles others have had
in your life as excuses for your mistakes.
Take control and live your own life.
Continue the journey you've begun,
which is inside of you.
It is the most difficult journey you'll ever make,
but the most rewarding.
Take strength from those you love,
and let those who love you help you.
Open up your heart; put aside your image
   and find your real self.
Keep your pride, but don't live for it.
Believe in your own goodness,
   and then do good things.
You are capable of them.

Work at being the you that you want to be.
Sacrifice desires of the moment for long-term goals.
The sacrifices will be for your benefit;
you will be proud of yourself.
As you approach life, be thankful
for all the good things that you have.
Be thankful for all the potential
    that you're blessed with.
Believe in that potential — and use it.
You are a wonderful person, so do wonderful things.
True happiness must come from within you.
You will find happiness by letting your conscience
    guide you —
        listen to it; follow it.
Your conscience is the key to your happiness.
Don't strive to impress others,
    but strive to impress yourself.
Be the person you were meant to be.
Everything else will follow;
    your dreams will come true.

— Karen Poynter Taylor

# May You Receive These Gifts Every Day

Freedom and honesty...

to truly get to know yourself and what you want in life.

Joy and wonder...

the kind you get from loving someone more deeply than you ever dreamed possible and the happiness of sharing life with them.

Strength and confidence...

the kind that comes from those experiences that teach you that you can rely on yourself and you do have something to say about your destiny.

Courage and energy...

to pursue the adventure of exploring your own dreams — big or small.

Tolerance, insight, and perspective...

to see others as they are and let them be, along with the gentle openness to learn from them and apply what you can to your own life, while still maintaining the values that are right for you.

Peace and happiness...

the kind that comes from knowing you are loved.

— Deeva D. Boleman

Many people
go from one thing
to another
searching for happiness
but with each new venture
they find themselves
more confused
and less happy
until they discover
that what they are
searching for
is inside themselves
and what will make them happy
is sharing their real selves
with the one they love

— Susan Polis Schutz

Love flows from the beauty
   around us
Love smiles through those
   we hold especially dear
Love speaks soft words
   that help guide us

— Joel Winsome Williams


The love we give away
is the only love we keep.

— Elbert Hubbard


And now abide faith,
hope, love, these three;
but the greatest of these
is love.

— 1 Corinthians 13:13 (NKJV)

# Desiderata

Go placidly amid the noise and the haste, and remember what peace there may be in silence. ➤ As far as possible, without surrender, be on good terms with all persons. Speak your truth quietly and clearly; and listen to others, even to the dull and ignorant; they too have their story. ➤ Avoid loud and aggressive persons; they are vexatious to the spirit. ➤ If you compare yourself with others, you may become vain or bitter, for always there will be greater and lesser persons than yourself. ➤ Enjoy your achievements as well as your plans. Keep interested in your own career, however humble; it is a real possession in the changing fortunes of time. ➤ Exercise caution in your business affairs, for the world is full of trickery. But let this not blind you to what virtue there is; many persons strive for high ideals, and everywhere life is full of heroism. ➤ Be yourself. Especially do not feign affection.

Neither be cynical about love; for in the face of all aridity and disenchantment, it is as perennial as the grass. ◆ Take kindly the counsel of the years, gracefully surrendering the things of youth. Nurture strength of spirit to shield you in sudden misfortune. But do not distress yourself with dark imaginings. Many fears are born of fatigue and loneliness. ◆ Beyond a wholesome discipline, be gentle with yourself. ◆ You are a child of the universe no less than the trees and the stars; you have a right to be here. ◆ And whether or not it is clear to you, no doubt the universe is unfolding as it should. Therefore be at peace with God, whatever you conceive Him to be. ◆ And whatever your labors and aspirations, in the noisy confusion of life, keep peace in your soul. ◆ With all its sham, drudgery and broken dreams, it is still a beautiful world. Be cheerful. Strive to be happy. ◆

— Max Ehrmann

Where your pleasure is, there is your treasure.
Where your treasure is, there is your heart.
Where your heart is, there is your happiness.

— St. Augustine

Be such a man, and live such a life, that if
every man were such as you, the earth would
be God's paradise.

— Phillips Brooks

Helping our fellowman is the rent for
the space we occupy on this earth —
the more rent you pay the greater will
be your happiness and joy in living.

— Anonymous

Write it on your heart that every day is the best day in the year. No man has learned anything rightly until he knows that every day is doomsday. Today is a king in disguise. Today always looks mean to the thoughtless, in the face of a uniform experience that all good and great and happy actions are made up precisely of these blank todays. Let us not be so deceived; let us unmask the king as he passes! He only is rich who owns the day, and no one owns the day who allows it to be invaded with worry, fret and anxiety. Finish every day and be done with it. You have done what you could. Some blunders and absurdities no doubt crept in; forget them as soon as you can. Tomorrow is a new day; begin it well and serenely and with too high a spirit to be cumbered with your old nonsense. This day is all that is good and fair. It is too dear, with its hopes and invitations, to waste a moment on the yesterdays.

— Ralph Waldo Emerson

# We Need to Feel More

We need to feel more to understand others
We need to love more to be loved back
We need to cry more to cleanse ourselves
We need to laugh more to enjoy ourselves

We need to establish the values of
honesty and fairness
when interacting with people
We need to establish a strong ethical basis
as a way of life

We need to see more
than our own little fantasies
We need to hear more
and listen to the needs of others

We need to give more and take less
We need to share more and own less
We need to realize the importance of the family
as a backbone to stability
We need to look more
and realize that we are not so different
from one another

We need to create a world where
we can all peacefully live
the life we choose
We need to create a world where
we can once again trust each other

— Susan Polis Schutz

39

There are nine requisites
   for contented living:
Health enough to make
   work a pleasure
Wealth enough
   to support your needs.
Strength enough to battle with
   difficulties and overcome them.
Grace enough to confess
   your sins and forsake them.
Patience enough to toil
   until some good is accomplished.
Charity enough to see
   some good in your neighbor.
Love enough to move you
   to be useful and helpful to others.
Faith enough to make real
   the things of God.
Hope enough to remove all
   anxious fears concerning the future.

— Johann Wolfgang von Goethe

i thank You God for most this amazing
day:for the leaping greenly spirits of trees
and a blue true dream of sky;and for everything
which is natural which is infinite which is yes

(i who have died am alive again today,
and this is the sun's birthday;this is the birth
day of life and of love and wings:and of the gay
great happening illimitably earth)

how should tasting touching hearing seeing
breathing any — lifted from the no
of all nothing — human merely being
doubt unimaginable You?

(now the ears of my ears awake and
now the eyes of my eyes are opened)

— E. E. Cummings

# Be Someone Who Knows
# What You Want in Life...

Not one of us can live merely by knowledge —
you have need to think.
What thoughts are there that you have need of?
You need to think about the true way
of being a human being,
not merely to be someone who has knowledge
or is clever in what he does;
but to be somebody
who knows what he wants to do.
Be one who knows that for life
you require the truth,
that to live you need goodness,
to live you need gratitude;
that within life there is a spiritual life
and that we are but poor if we go into life
without a realization of that spiritual life.

— Albert Schweitzer

Everything that's ever happened to me has been the result of faith. The faith I found in my father's house, and now find in my own house, and in my world. Sure, there are different beliefs, but as long as men believe, they believe basically the same thing. The lyrics may be different, but the music is always the same.

— Perry Como

Faith is to believe what we do not see; and the reward of this faith is to see what we believe.

— St. Augustine

Know that the greatest things which are done on earth are done within, in the hearts of faithful souls.

— St. Louis de Montfort

I open up the door to greet
the early morning sun,
Closing it behind me and away I do run
To the meadow where the meadowlark
is singing in the trees,
In the meadow I go walking
in the early morning breeze.

Misty-eyed I look about
the meadow where I stray;
It's there I find the courage
to greet the coming day.
For there among the flowers
I kneel gently to my knees
To have a word with God
in the early morning breeze.

— Dolly Parton

# God Is Always
# with You

In times of change and crisis,
may love speak to you
     and bring you comfort.
May hope remind you
     that in this life and beyond
God is always with you.

Hope comes when we trust God
with the things we cannot
     understand.
Even when we cannot see it,
He is at work in our lives —
lending a helping hand,
listening to each problem,
comforting and healing our hearts.

God doesn't run away
     from our need;
He runs toward it.
On the days when there is no light,
He is the loving promise
that the light will come again.

— Linda E. Knight

# Make Each and Every Moment of Your Life a Moment to Remember

Be a person who likes virtually everything about life — who is comfortable doing just about anything, and who wastes no time complaining or wishing that things were otherwise ➤ Be enthusiastic about life, and want all you can get out of it ➤ Refuse to worry, and keep yourself free from the anxiety that accompanies worry ➤ Live now, rather than in the past or the future ➤ Seek out experiences that are new and unfamiliar to you ➤ Be strikingly independent ➤ Treasure your own freedom from expectations, and want those you love to be independent, to make their own choices, and to live their lives for themselves ➤ Know how to laugh, and how to create laughter ➤ Accept yourself without complaint ➤ Appreciate the natural world ➤ Enjoy being outdoors in nature and tripping around all that is unspoiled and original ➤ Have insight into the behavior of others, and into yourself, too ➤ Never feel threatened ➤ Engage in work that will make other people's lives more pleasant or tolerable ➤ Treat your body well ➤ Be honest ➤ Have little concern with order, organization, or systems in your life ➤ Be creative ➤ Love life and all the activities in it ➤ Be aggressively curious ➤ Search for more to learn each and every present moment of your life ➤ Do not be afraid to fail; in fact, welcome it! ➤ Do not equate being successful in any enterprise with being successful as a human being ➤ Accept others as they are, and work at changing events that you dislike ➤ View all people as human, and place no one above yourself in importance ➤ Don't chase after happiness; live and happiness is your payoff.

— Dr. Wayne W. Dyer

# It's Okay

It's okay to be afraid
of the things you don't understand.
It's okay to feel anxious
when things aren't working your way.
It's okay to feel lonely...
even when you're with other people.
It's okay to feel unfulfilled
because you know something is missing
(even if you're not sure what it is).
It's okay to think and worry and cry.

It's okay to do
whatever you have to do, but
just remember, too,
that eventually you're going to
adjust to the changes life brings your way,
and you'll realize that
it's okay to love again and laugh again,
and it's okay to get to the point where
the life you live
is full and satisfying and good to you...
and it will be that way
because you made it that way.

— Laine Parsons

# When You Follow Your Own Heart, the Choices You Make Will Always Be the Right Ones

What you do with your life
is your own choice.
How you decide to live your life
and achieve your goals is up to you,
and no one but you.
Mistakes will be made,
but you can learn from your mistakes.

Always remember to live your life
in a way that's right for you.
Everything you do should make you happy,
and those who may at first disagree
will hopefully, in time,
be happy for you, too.
Then you will come to see
that the choices you make are right —
if you make them for yourself.

— Jodi R. Ernst

True happiness comes not from external
things, but through attachment to things
spiritual. It is an inner joy which nothing
outside can destroy. It comes from God
and is a reward for goodness.

— Bhagavad Gita

Goodness and love... cause the joy
and beauty of love to shine forth
from every part of the face. When
this form of love is seen, it appears
ineffably beautiful, and affects with
delight the inmost life of the soul.

— E. Swedenborg


The best creed
we can have
is charity towards
the creeds of others.

— Josh Billings

# Let Your Spirit
# Shine Through!

You have an inner jewel. Let your spirit, the divine gem, shine through, and create a radiance about you wherever you go.

Let your mind be planted with seeds of love and joy and hope, and courage and universal goodwill and opulent harvest shall grow.

Think of each year as a sower scattering these seeds in your heart; then water them with the dews of sympathy, and throw open the windows to the broad sunlight of heaven while they ripen.

And — as surely as the days
come and go —

so surely
shall your
life grow.

— Ella Wheeler Wilcox

Look to this day
for it is life
the very life of life
In its brief course lie all
the realities and truths of existence
the joy of growth
the splendor of action
the glory of power
For yesterday is but a memory
And tomorrow is only a vision
But today well lived
makes every yesterday a memory
of happiness
and every tomorrow a vision of hope
Look well, therefore, to this day!

— Ancient Sanskrit Poem

If I had my life to live over,
I would relax more.
I wouldn't take so many things
so seriously.
I would take more chances.
I would climb more mountains,
and swim more rivers...
Next time
I'd start barefooted
earlier in the spring
and stay that way
later in the fall.
I wouldn't make such good grades
unless I enjoyed working for them.
I'd go to more dances.
I'd ride on more merry-go-rounds.
I'd pick more daisies.

— Nadine Stair

Always remember to forget
the things that made you sad,
but never forget to remember
the things that made you glad.

— Elbert Hubbard

What lies behind us
and what lies
before us are
tiny matters
compared to what
lies within us.

— Ralph Waldo Emerson

# My Creed

To live as gently as I can;
To be, no matter where, a man;
To take what comes of good or ill
And cling to faith and honor still;
To do my best, and let that stand
The record of my brain and hand;
And then, should failure come to me,
Still work and hope for victory.

To have no secret place wherein
I stoop unseen to shame or sin;
To be the same when I'm alone
As when my every deed is known;
To live undaunted, unafraid
Of any step that I have made;
To be without pretense or sham
Exactly what men think I am.

To leave some simple mark behind
To keep my having lived in mind;
If enmity to aught I show,
To be an honest, generous foe,
To play my little part, nor whine
That greater honors are not mine.
This, I believe, is all I need
For my philosophy and creed.

— Edgar A. Guest

# Gentle Words of Encouragement

Spend every day preparing for the next.

As you reach forward with one hand, accept the advice of those who have gone before you, and in the same manner reach back with the other hand to those who follow you; for life is a fragile chain of experiences held together by love. Take pride in being a strong link in that chain. Discipline yourself, but do not be harsh. The pleasures of life are yours to be taken. Share them with others, but always remember that you, too, have earned the right to partake.

Know those who love you; love is the finest of all gifts and is received only to be given. Embrace those who truly love you; for they are few in a lifetime. Then return that love tenfold, radiating it from your heart to fill their lives as sunlight warms the darkest corners of the earth. Love is a journey, not a destination; travel its path daily. Do this and your troubles will be as fleeting as footprints in the sand. When loneliness is your companion and all about you seem to be gone, pause and listen, for the sound of loneliness is silence, and in silence we hear best. Listen well, and your moments of silence will always be broken by the gentle words of encouragement spoken by those of us who love you.

— Tim Murtaugh

# Acceptance

Acceptance means that you
   can find the serenity within
to let go of the past
   with its mistakes and regrets,
move into the future
   with a new perspective,
and appreciate the opportunity
   to take a second chance.

Acceptance means you'll find
   security again
when difficult times come
   into your life,
and comfort to relieve any pain.
You'll find new dreams, fresh hopes,
and forgiveness of the heart.

Acceptance does not mean
   that you will always be perfect.
It simply means that
   you'll always overcome imperfection.

Acceptance is the road to peace —
   letting go of the worst,
holding on to the best,
   and finding the hope inside
that continues throughout life.

Acceptance
   is the heart's best defense,
love's greatest asset,
   and the easiest way
      to keep believing
in yourself and others.

— Regina Hill

# May You Always Feel Loved

May you find serenity and tranquility in a world you may not always understand. May the pain you have known and the conflict you have experienced give you the strength to walk through life facing each new situation with courage and optimism. Always know that there are those whose love and understanding will always be there, even when you feel most alone. May you discover enough goodness in others to believe in a world of peace. May a kind word, a reassuring touch, and a warm smile be yours every day of your life, and may you give these gifts as well as receive them. Remember the sunshine when the storm seems unending. Teach love to those who know hate, and let that love embrace you as you go into the world. May the teachings of those you admire become part of you, so that you may call upon them. Remember, those whose lives you have touched and who

have touched yours are always a part of you,
even if the encounters were less than you would
have wished. It is the content of the encounter
that is more important than its form. May you
not become too concerned with material matters,
but instead place immeasurable value on the
goodness in your heart. Find time in each day to
see beauty and love in the world around you.
Realize that each person has limitless abilities, but
each of us is different in our own way. What you
may feel you lack in one regard may be more than
compensated for in another. What you feel you
lack in the present may become one of your
strengths in the future. May you see your future
as one filled with promise and possibility. Learn to
view everything as a worthwhile experience. May you
find enough inner strength to determine your
own worth by yourself, and not be dependent on
another's judgment of your accomplishments. May
you always feel loved.

— Sandra Sturtz Hauss

Touch the sky
and in your reach
believe
　achieve
　　and aspire.

May your tomorrows
take you to the
summit of your goals

　And your joys
　take you
　even higher.

　　　— Douglas Pagels


May you look upon the future
　secure in your strength
　　and sustained by your faith.
As you embrace changes,
　let your dreams soar —
Knowing only the limits
　of your own imagination!

　　　— Norma Noraker McGihon

# ACKNOWLEDGMENTS

We gratefully acknowledge the permission granted by the following authors, publishers, and authors' representatives to reprint poems or excerpts from their publications.

Robert L. Bell for "Desiderata" by Max Ehrmann. Copyright © 1927 by Max Ehrmann. All rights reserved. Reprinted by permission of Robert L. Bell, Melrose, Massachusetts 02176.

Susan Polis Schutz for "We Need to Feel More." Copyright © 1972 by Continental Publications. All rights reserved. From the book I'M NOT THAT KIND OF GIRL, published by Blue Mountain Press. Used by permission.

Liveright Publishing Corporation for "I thank You God for this most amazing," by E. E. Cummings. Copyright © 1950, 1978, 1991 by the Trustees for the E. E. Cummings Trust. Copyright © 1979 by George James Firmage, from COMPLETE POEMS: 1904-1962 by E. E. Cummings, Edited by George J. Firmage. All rights reserved. Reprinted by permission.

Albert Schweitzer Foundation, Inc. for "Be Someone Who Knows What You Want in Life..." by Albert Schweitzer. Copyright © 1987 by the Albert Schweitzer Foundation, Inc. All rights reserved. Reprinted by permission.

Guideposts Magazine for "Everything that's ever happened..." from NO TAX ON MY HEART by Perry Como. Copyright © 1953 by Guideposts, Carmel, New York 10512. All rights reserved. Reprinted by permission.

Velvet Apple Music for "I open up the door..." by Dolly Parton. From the song, THE EARLY MORNING BREEZE. Copyright © 1970 by Velvet Apple Music. All rights reserved. Reprinted by permission.

Dr. Wayne W. Dyer for "Make Each and Every Moment of Your Life a Moment to Remember" from YOUR ERRONEOUS ZONES by Dr. Wayne W. Dyer. Copyright © 1976 by Wayne W. Dyer. All rights reserved. Reprinted by permission.

Regnery Publishing for "My Creed" from COLLECTED VERSE by Edgar A. Guest. Copyright © 1934 by Regnery Publishing. All rights reserved. Reprinted by special permission of Regnery Publishing, Inc., Washington, D.C.

A careful effort has been made to trace the ownership of poems and excerpts used in this anthology in order to obtain permission to reprint copyrighted materials and give proper credit to the copyright owners. If any error or omission has occurred, it is completely in advertent, and we would like to make corrections in future editions provided that written notification is made to the publisher:

BLUE MOUNTAIN PRESS, INC., P.O. Box 4549, Boulder, Colorado 80306